Aman Dag Naud

The Wonderful French Riviera

Photographs by Hervé Boulé

Translated by Angela Moyon

EDITIONS OUEST-FRANCE
13 rue du Breil, Rennes

Top : *The casino in Monte-Carlo*

Middle : *The village of Peille, which has kept its mediaeval atmosphere.*

Bottom : *View from the Esterel Corniche, or scenic route.*

Front cover : *Aerial view of Saint-Tropez.*

Back cover : *The Monaco Rock seen from the tropical gardens.*

Sainte-Maxime.

INTRODUCTION

Two hundred years ago, Monaco was a small village, Cannes a poverty-stricken fishing port, and Nice had a population of no more than twelve thousand. The journey from Paris took twelve days and was difficult and often dangerous. The Esterel was a favourite haunt of bandits and the R. Var, which formed the frontier between France and Savoy, was forded on the backs of the ferrymen because there was no bridge!

On 24th March 1860, the County of Nice was annexed to France. Trains began to run down to the coast and, in 1887, the travel writer Stephen Liegeard published a work called "The French Riviera". The name stuck. But visitors were few in number and all belonged to the privileged classes. These were the days of palaces built for English aristocrats, Russian princes, and the first American millionaires. When the French President, Félix Faure, passed through the region in 1896, he met the former British Prime Minister Gladstone in Cannes, the Russian Crown Prince in Nice, Prince Albert of Belgium in Monaco, and Emperor Franz Joseph of Austria in Menton.

The Riviera only came alive in the winter. People with private incomes and those suffering from tuberculosis came to enjoy the clement weather, the beautiful scenery, and the exotic profusion of plant life. Then sea bathing became fashionable. Without being convinced that it was the right decision, hoteliers began to keep their establishments open in the summer months as from 2nd August 1931. Hordes of "sun-seeking" tourists arrived, and bathers crowded onto the beaches. The fine forest of pines, oaks, and olive trees began to be infested with concrete bungalows and stretches of motorway. Wide areas of blackened stumps are reminders of past fires. "The Wonderful Riviera" - or is it?

In the following pages, we should like to look behind the scenes. The Riviera has had its share of History's troubles - barbarian invasions, Saracen raids, plague epidemics, earthquakes, and property speculation. But it has never lost its hold on life. One of the caves on the Corniche was inhabited by a woman, perhaps as much as 250.000 years ago.

Six hundred years before Christianity came to the world, Greek merchants plied their trade in the ports of Antipolis (Antibes), Nikaïa (Nice) and Monoikos (Monaco). The area has many precious reminders of the Roman occupation - the arena in Fréjus, town walls in Antibes, Roman baths in Cimiez etc. The fortifications and hilltop villages have stood firm against attack from feudal armies. Even the forest springs back to life after repeated decimation by fire.

This vitality can be explained by the region's infinite diversity. After the creeks in the Esterel come the long beaches in Cannes and Fréjus. In winter, the Mercantour can be having temperatures of - 20°C. while people stroll along the Croisette in their shirt sleeves. In the high mountains behind Nice, each valley and village has its own character. The language of the troubadours can still be heard there to this day.

In Saint-Tropez, modest fishermen don't bat an eyelid when they rub shoulders with stars well-known to the general public. In Monte-Carlo, the pinball machines in the cafés are just two steps away from the roulette tables where fortunes are lost. The "new-style cuisine" served in luxurious restaurants has not replaced the traditional bouillabaisse (fish stew), aïoli (garlic mayonnaise) and pissaladiera (quiche containing anchovy paste), nor the less grand wines from Bandol and Saint-Jeannet. The same is true of crafts. Glazed earthenware from Moustiers, pottery from Vallauris, perfume from Grasse, and woven textiles from Tourrette all exist side by side with high tech industries in

The rock on which the town of Monaco is built.

Scenery round the Madonna of Utelle.

Sophia Antipolis and La Gaude, once the homeland of the writer Pagnol.

It takes exceptional strength to face up to all these contrasts and the local people draw on the omnipresent traditions that have been but little obscured by the hustle and bustle of tourism. Brotherhoods of penitents still process with their heads hooded. St. Agnes has her chapel on the hills above Menton, St. Dévote is in Monaco, Réparate is to be found in Nice, and St. Honorat and his sister Margaret keep watch over the island of Lérins. In Vence, the painter Matisse has brought his own form of light to present-day spirituality.

From the Carnival in Nice to the Monaco Grand Prix, from the homely game of bowls to the Cannes Film Festival, there is a common thread running through everything - a sense of festivity and hospitality. It is the cricket that is king, not the ant as it was in the fable. Friendship is established at once and refusals are categorical. When the Turks, who were allied to the French, climbed the walls of Nice in 1543, Catherine Ségurane was waiting for them with her washerwoman's paddle. Then she turned her back on them and lifted her skirts.

You have to take the Riviera as it is, with its faults and its marvels. Artists have understood this and have found new sources of inspiration in Vence or Nice. The ''noses'' of the perfume industry discover new fragrances in the orange groves of Vallauris, the carnations of Menton, the roses of Antibes and the mimosas of Mandelieu. This is the French Riviera - a scent, a quality of light, buildings and men that are worth taking time to get to know.

5

Hyères, the former Collegiate Church of St.Paul.

◁*A fountain in the new districts of Hyères.*

HYÈRES

Hyères, the Olbia of the Ancient Greeks, has two faces. Along the seafront is the lower town, the haunt of the "strangers" i.e. the tourists. The old town on the hilltop still has a feudal appearance. Just take a look at the ruins and crenelated walls of the castle where St. Louis once stayed. And the Rade, Princes and Fenouillet Gates. The houses twisted by the passing years. The 12th-century St. Blaise' Tower. The old colleigate church of St. Paul, which also dates from the 12th century, and St. Louis' Church, formerly the chapel in the Franciscan Friary (13th century).

The Giens Peninsula jutting out into the sea is a geographical oddity. Two narrow sandbanks have been pushed together by the currents until they finally linked the island of Giens to the continent. They border the Pesquiers salt marshes, the only salt marsh still worked on the Riviera.

The Fondue Tower at the tip of the Giens peninsula.

ISLANDS OF PORQUEROLLES AND PORT-CROS

Offshore from the Giens Peninsula stands a group of rocky islets that were, for many years, known as the Iles d'Or (Golden Isles). Porquerolles, which is covered with pine trees and heather, is almost 4 1/2 miles long and 1 mile wide. Its strategic importance is obvious from the fortresses. It stands on sentry duty and, on its southernmost tip, there is a lighthouse with a range of more than 30 miles.

Port-Cros, which is almost 3 miles long, is more wild and rugged. It was designated as a National Park in 1963. Its 640 hectares are now a nature reserve, and a paradise for butterflies and birds. There are even herring gulls and shags on the island. It is irrigated by twelve springs and its vegetation is lush and green. Fig trees, palms and eucalytpus grow in abundance. The scrub is denser than elsewhere and the cork-oak forest is thicker. This is why smoking, hunting and camping are prohibited on Port-Cros.

The sea round about is also a protected environment, to a distance of 650 yds. Motor boats and underwater fishing are not permitted. But you may dive to try and locate the dolphins, monk seals, or turtles that haunt these waters.

Top : *The Cap d'Arme on the south coast of Porquerolles.*

Bottom : *Porquerolles harbour.*

On previous page :
The main beach on Porquerolles.

10

Scenery in the Maures.

THE MAURES RANGE

The Maures Range, ancient hills of granite, gneiss and schist with an average altitude of 1,300 ft. is the land of pine trees, cork-oaks, chestnuts, and scrub where heather and arbuthus abound. It is thought to have got its name not from the Saracens who frequently raided this part of the coast, but from the Provençal word "Maouro" which describes dark woods.

The coast between the Giens and Saint-Tropez Peninsulas, indeed down to Saint-Aygulf, is broken up by sheltered natural harbours - Bormes-les-Mimosas, Pramousquier, Cavalaire, and Saint-Tropez itself.

Inland, the hairpin bends take you from ravines up to cols, and from picturesque villages that still have their original appearance to mysterious hermitages like the Carthusian monastery in La Verne founded in 1171, or Notre-Dame-des-Anges that stands almost at the top of the Maures, an ancient hermitage in honour of St. Nymphe, a young Italian girl who suffered martyrdom in Rome during the first centuries of Christianity. From the terrace, there is a view over the port of Toulon, the Sainte-Baume mountain, the Mediterranean, and, in the distance, Corsica.

Bormes-les-Mimosas.

The coastline along the Maures.

NOTRE-DAME DE LA VERNE

The Carthusian monastery of Notre-Dame de La Verne, which is a glimpse of eternity, was built in 1171 on a rocky spur in the Maures deep in the heart of scrub emblazoned with chestnut trees that are hundreds of years old. It was fortified to withstand attack by pillaging hordes, altered after the Wars of Religion, and abandoned during the French Revolution. Yet the ruins of the monastery still seem to vibrate with the strains of some mysterious prayer. Perhaps it is because of the stone that was used in the building - black- and green-streaked serpentine.

A 16th-century monumental gateway opens onto the monastic close. Round the courtyard are the

The Carthusian monastery of La Verne (photo by J.P. Gisserot).

outhouses, stables, bakery, and guesthouse. Above all, there is a fine 12th-century kitchen. Another gate opens onto the monastery itself. First come the small cloisters, then the Romanesque chapel and the great cloisters bordered by the monks' accommodation (four rooms and a small garden for each brother).

Outside the walls, on the platform on the north side overlooking the Maures, a windmill stands as if on sentry duty.

The main serpentine gateway.

SAINT-TROPEZ

For many years, Saint-Tropez was only connected to the rest of Provence by the Pine Cone Train, so-called because the passengers got out as the train climbed the Maures and gathered pine cones to feed the fire in the old locomotive. These were the happy days of artists like Signac and Bonnard, who so loved this quiet little harbour dominated by the massive fortress with its 16th-century towers.

Then came the darlings of the Parisian Smart Set - Mistinguett, Maurice Chevalier, and later Brigitte Bardot in her "Madrague". The yachts replaced the fishing smacks. But as you stroll near the harbour, in the streets of old pink houses around the 19th-century Baroque church, you will find something of the French Riviera of times past.

The Graniers Beach on the other side of the fortress and the Salins, Tahiti and Pampelonne beaches with their beautiful fine sand are a haven for nudists. But you may prefer the more modest exhibitions in the Annonciade Museum near the Quai de l'Epi. It houses a few masterpieces by artists who stayed in Saint-Tropez - Signac and Bonnard of course, but also Marquet, Van Dongen, Derain, Matisse and Maillol.

The Quai Jean-Jaurès in Saint-Tropez.

On previous page and below : *Aerial views of Saint-Tropez.*

The hilltop village of Ramatuelle.

RAMATUELLE

In the last century, Ramatuelle was an isolated, secretive, rather wild place. "Its low black houses, narrow streets, some of them very steep, make it a very dismal place to look at and an equally dismal place to stay. The people are hard-working and sober-minded but they are rather backward as regards civilisation." (E. Garcin - *Dictionnaire historique et topo-graphique de la Provence* - 1835).

The mystery later became the subject of society gossip with a whiff of scandal to it on the heights of Ramatuelle. Yet until 1985, the twisted elm tree planted on the square in the days of Sully's administration, provided the bowls-players with some shade. And on one of the grave-stones in the cemetery is an ins-cription that is moving for its very simplicity - "Gérard Philipe -

4 décembre 1922 - 25 novembre 1959''. The actor who played Fanfan la Tulipe has been laid to rest here.

Beyond the Col de Paillas not far from the village are three rui-ned windmills and a radio mast, on a promontory from which there is a panoramic view of the coastline below the Maures, the Esterel, and across the Alps to the north-east.

Aerial view of Port-Grimaud.

PORT-GRIMAUD

Port-Grimaud is built round a manmade lake and was designed by François Spoerry in the 1960's. With its canals, its yellow ochre, pink, and white houses, its narrow streets and its tiny "piazzas", you might imagine yourself in the Venetian lagoon, in a town identical to Burano. Waterbuses ply their trade here like the vaporetti in Venice, because cars are prohibited.

LE THORONET

Le Thoronet is the apotheosis of the serenity and mystery expressed by the other two Cistercian architectural gems in Provence - Sénanque and Silvacane.

Lying in the depths of an isolated valley between Brignoles and Vidauban, the abbey fascinates visitors because of its austerity and the purity of its Romanesque architecture. The church, cloisters and monastery buildings were built between 1176 and 1190. Only the chapter house dates from the Gothic period. Its palm-ribbed vaulting is supported by two pillars whose capitals are carved with plant motifs. These are the only carvings in the abbey.

The cloisters are outstanding for the thickness of the walls in the semi-circular arcading. In each arch are twin lights and a tympanum containing an oculus. At one end of the cloisters is a small hexagonal building used by the monks as a lavabo, or wash-room. It is the only one still in existence in France.

Each section of the abbey (church, cloisters, chapter house, monks' room, refectory, library, parlour, and dormitory) corresponds to one of the eight hours of monastic prayer. In fact, the entire community was designed like a gigantic sundial.

The majesty and pure architectural lines of the church in Le Thoronet.

◁ *Arcading in the cloisters.*

19

Glazed earthenware from Moustiers-Sainte-Marie (photo by J.Bernard, F.Morin).

MOUSTIERS-SAINTE-MARIE

Moustiers-Sainte-Marie is an excellent point of departure for trips to the Verdon. It is also a pleasant place in stay. It lies in an amazing location at the mouth of a breach in the limestone cliff worn away by a rushing river, the Rioul. A wrought-iron chain 738 ft. long from which hangs a gilded star joins the sheer sides of the cliff. It was given to the town by a Knight Crusader, Baron de Blacas, who was miraculously freed from a Saracen gaol thanks to the intercession of Our Lady of Beauvoir.

The narrow streets, some of them broken up by flights of steps, wend their way past the pottery shops. The first glazed earthenware dishes were made by Pierre I de Clérissy in 1679. Since then, numerous master craftsmen have worked in Moustiers - Joseph Olérys, Fouque, the Ferrat Brothers, the decorator Féraud, Marcel Provence in 1925 and Simone Garnier. All of them are represented in the Pottery Museum housed in a mediaeval crypt.

A couple of yards away is the church with its massive traceried belltower. It has a Romanesque nave and a fine Gothic chancel.

Perched on a hilltop above the town is the chapel of Our Lady of Beauvoir, an ancient place of pilgrimage founded after the visit of St. Sidoine Apollinaire in the 5th century. A path leads up to it, flanked by fourteen oratories that are, in fact, Stations of the Cross. The present building, which dates from the 12th century, underwent alteration in the 16th. On the chapel door is the inscription, "Belvisura vocor : diffundit lumina nomen", which means "I am the Virgin Mary of Beauvoir. As my name says, I bring a new light" - for the Virgin Mary of Beauvoir gave sight back to the blind and brought stillborn babies back to life.

THE VERDON

The Grand Canyon of the Verdon is one of the most impressive beauty spots anywhere in the world. The river, which is a tributary of the R.Durance, is imprisoned between sheer walls of limestone where the drop varies from 650 ft. to 2,275 ft. Only the Colorado is comparable to it.

Leave Moustiers-Sainte-Marie by the D 952 road that follows the north bank of the Verdon. There are observation platforms at Galetas, Mayreste which is accessible on foot only, and at the Col d'Ayen. On your right as you enter La Palud, you will see the D 23 which is the start of the hilltop route completed in 1973. It leads to a winding road high above the gorge, at the Maline observation platforms. Far below, the R. Verdon occasionally disappears from view beneath falls of rock. A long-distance way-marked footpath, the GR 4, starts from the Chalet Martel and leads along the floor of the canyon to the Point Sublime. It is a long hike, at least six hours' walking over what can be difficult terrain when the path becomes a mere footbridge across cracks in the rock or a ladder up the rock face in the Samson Gully.

The winding D 23 road runs close to the edge of the precipice. A stop at the Glacières observation platform is a must, because of the view over the Mescla where the green waters of the rivers Verdon and Artuby come together. And don't miss the Tilleul, l'Escalès and Trescaïre viewpoints. The Hilltop Route rejoins the D 952. The Point Sublime overlooks a gigantic and seemingly bottomless crack in the rock with strangely-formed sides. Gliding above the gorge are birds of prey, rock swallows, and jackdaws, all of them making the best of thermal currents. Climb to Rougon, a veritable eyrie, before heading for Pont-de-Soleils.

From there, the D 955 and D 90 roads lead to the Balcons de la Mescla, the entrance to the Corniche Sublime which follows the left bank of the torrent. The single-span Artuby Bridge crosses the almost casually-formed precipice with its vertical walls of rock.

The Verdon Gorge seen from the Galetas observation platform (photo by M.Chanteux).

At the Fayet tunnels, there is a drop of 1,462 ft. A short distance away is the Restaurant des Cavaliers whose terrace stands high above one of the narrowest sections of the canyon.

Beyond Le Pas de l'Imbut, the road leaves the edge of the gorge, follows the wooded corrie of Vaumale, and arrives at the Col d'Illoire back at the entrance to the canyon.

FRÉJUS

Fréjus, the oldest of the towns on the French Riviera, was originally a seaport. The old quays can be seen from the top of the Saint-Antoine hill. But the harbour silted up before finally being filled in, in 1782. Despite destruction by the Moors in the 10th century, later wars and pillaging, the air raids of August 1944, and the collapse of the Malpasset Dam on 2nd December 1959 (which caused 423 deaths), the town has preserved a number of prestigious ancient and mediaeval buildings.

Of the Roman Fréjus, or Forum Julii described by Cicero, there remain the arena that once catered for ten thousand spectators, a few walls of the theatre, the Orée Gate, remnants of the town walls, the Western and Eastern citadels (Saint-Antoine hill and Plateforme), and a fine 25-mile aquaduct which brought water down from the Siagnole.

The mediaeval streets or vennels with their central gutters all converge on the fortified cathedral built in the 10th century on the site once occupied by a temple to Jupiter. The 4th-5th century baptistery, which is one of the oldest in France, is separated from the

Top : *The cloisters in Fréjus.*

Bottom :
The ruins of a Roman aquaduct.

Aerial view of Saint-Raphaël.

nave by a porch. Adjacent to the cathedral are the 12th - 13th century cloisters, which are unusual for their galleries with wooden ceilings. In the 15th century, these ceilings were decorated with animals and monsters.

SAINT-RAPHAËL

Nestling against the Esterel, bathed by the waters of the R. Garonne, and caressed by the sea along the entire length of its fine sandy beach, Saint-Raphaël is a pleasant summer holiday resort. It is more of a family resort than either Cannes or Saint-Tropez, with attractive walks along the seafront, on the jetties of the old harbour, near the casino and on the Cours René-Coty. Offshore, in the shelter of twin red reefs called the Land Lion and the Sea Lion, there is said to be a sunken town. At certain times of the year, the bells are said to be heard ringing beneath the sea.

The original village of Saint-Raphaël developed inland around the church dedicated to the archangel Raphael and to St. Peter. This strange building, which was started in the 12th century, was built in the Provençal Romanesque style and has massive piers. Like the Bishop's Palace, of which only a few ruins remain, the church was a place of refuge during raids by the Saracen. The neighbouring house has been turned into a museum where there is an exhibition of treasures discovered during local digs along the seabed.

Bonaparte landed here on his return from Egypt on 9th October 1799, and found it to be a charming fishing village. In the 19th century, the journalist Alphonse Karr settled here, bringing in his wake the Parisian Smart Set - Dumas, Maupassant, Berlioz and, later, Gounod. Since then, hotels have replaced the cosy houses, and stretches of bare concrete mask the "wishy-washy" decoration on a few fine villas (e.g. "Roquerousse", 167 boulevard de la Libération).

The Esterel Corniche.

Two views of the Esterel range. ▷

THE ESTEREL

Seen from the sea, the Esterel has some wonderful pink porphyry cliffs. Tourists in a hurry drive along the Corniche d'Or (Golden Cornice) from Saint-Raphaël to Cannes. They first pass the Pointe du Dramont of purplish rhyolite rocks and the Ile d'Or, an advanced guard topped by a tower. Once past the village of Agay that nestles at the head of the natural harbour, they see the volcanic rock of Saint-Barthélemy rising before them. A flight of steps cut into the red rhyolite runs up to the top, from which there is a birds' eye view of the gulfs, coves and reefs. Another signposted path leads to the summit of Cap Roux 1470 ft. above the sea, the remnants of a volcano from which there is a panoramic view.

The road drops down sharply to the Pointe de l'Observatoire where a concrete bunker juts out over the sea. It then runs on from creek to cove, passes the village of Trayas, and reaches Miramar and the Pointe de l'Esquilon from which there is a superb view. Finally, it arrives in La Napoule, on the edge of the Esterel.

Drivers with a more venturesome turn of mind leave Saint-Raphaël by the Valescure road and head for the Pic de l'Ours (1612 ft.). All round about are oak and pine forests that were decimated during fires in 1943, 1964 and 1986. But the heather, broom and lavender have covered them in splashes of colour. The road comes back down from the north via the Col de la Cadière and Les Suivières, and the Col de la Belle-Barbe which is the entrance to the impressive Mal Infernet, before finally reaching Valescure or Agay.

Why not let yourself be tempted by the countless footpaths that run through the forest in all directions. Near Mont Vinaigre (2008 ft.), the highest peak in the Esterel, not far from the Nationale 7 road, you can see the remains of the Roman villas of Roussivau or Grenouiller, the cobbles that formed the foundations of the Aurelian Way which leads from Italy to Arles via Antibes and Fréjus, the hermitages of the mystics of yesteryear, and the haunt of the 18th-century bandit

Gaspard de Besse, who used to seek refuge in the caves on Mont Vinaigre and in the inn in Les Adrets.

GRASSE

Grasse is the capital of perfume and crystallised fruit ; it is also an old Provençal town built in terraces up the hillside of Roquevignon, in the hinterland behind Cannes where marble, alabaster and jasper quarries abound. The mild climate, scent of the flowers, narrow winding streets and many fountains all attract tourists and those taking the waters. Pauline Bonaparte spent the winter of 1807-1808 here and Queen Victoria once stayed in the Grand Hôtel.

Le Puy, at the very top of the town, combines all the symbols of religious and political power. The former Bishop's Palace, now the Town Hall, is flanked by a auburn tuffstone tower dating from the

12th century. Notre-Dame "cathedral", which was built in the late 12th century in the Lombardy-Romanesque style, was restored in the 17th century. It has some outstanding furnishings - the St. Honorat reliquary (15th century), the "Washing of the Disciples' Feet", one of the few sacred works by the artist Fragonard, a triptych attributed to Louis Bréa, and three Rubens.

The old town was classified as a "listed district" in 1974. Guided tours take visitors round the old houses that once belonged to tanners and perfumers, the 15th- and 16th-century arcades, a corbelled house (Rue de l'Evêché), the Mont-de-Piété, and the famous Place aux Aires which was laid out in the 14th century.

The Museum of Provençal Art and History, which is housed in the 18th-century residence of the Marquis de Clapiers-Cabris who was related to the Marquis de Mirabeau, deals with popular traditions. It has some interesting collections of Christmas cribs, figurines, and comfit boxes (painted cardboard boxes).

The Place aux Aires and its flower market.

The Villa Fragonard on the Cours is a reminder of the famous painter who was born in Grasse in 1732. The villa belonged to his friend, the glover-perfumer Maubert, who provided him with accommodation during the French Revolution.

On left :

Top :
Grasse, the Museum of Provençal Art and History.

Bottom :
The nave of the Cathedral of Notre-Dame-du-Puy.

A fountain near the Place de la Foux.

27

CANNES

The Carlton, the Hôtel Royal, the Palm Beach, the old and new Festival Halls, the prestigious Croisette that runs along the shores of the gulf - this is elegant Cannes.

It was the British who made its fortune, the first of them being Lord Brougham, formerly Chancellor to Her Gracious Majesty, who was held up in the town when on his way to Nice in 1834. He fell in love with the little harbour full of reeds (or "cannes" hence the resort's name). He returned every winter and was soon imitated by the international smart set. Today, the International Film Festival, the Marché du Disque (MIDEM), and the Mimosa Festival in February, attract thousands of professionals and tourists from all over the world.

It takes a walk beneath the tall palm trees of the Croisette between the Palm Beach and the harbour (a mile-long stroll midway between the luxury hotels and their private beaches) to learn something of the luxurious poetry that is Cannes.

Once a Roman fort overlooking the harbour, the Suquet Hill forms the historical and popular heart of the town. The 12th-century Square Tower on the Mont Chevalier served as a lookout post. The belltower of Notre-Dame-d'Espérance (Our Lady of Hope) seems to keep watch over the town and the yachts. Finally, the La Castre Museum bears witness to people everywhere with its ethnological collections from every continent.

Cannes is surrounded by hills from which there are some wonderful panoramic views. To the west, the Croix des Gardes is

Above : *the observation platform in Super-Cannes.*

Opposite : *Views of La Croisette.*

533 ft. high. The California to the east has terraces of luxury villas. And Super-Cannes (alt. 1,056 ft.) seems to catch the sun's rays in its Observatory.

THE LÉRINS ISLES

"I love and honour my dear Lérins. It offers refuge to those who have just escaped this world's shipwrecks, providing shade for those who have been burned by the searing heat of our century... It is full of tumbling streams, leafy trees, and highly-scented flowers." The two Lérins Isles, Sainte-Marguerite and Saint-Honorat, which form an ageless, mysterious setting, have maintained all the serenity that was so greatly appreciated by St. Eucher more than fifteen hundred years ago.

It takes only a quarter of an hour, the length of the boat trip, to forget the hustle and bustle of Cannes. The boat ties up at the foot of the Royal Fortress in Sainte-Marguerite. On the left is the Ruelle des Cabanons, which climbs to the citadel built on Richelieu's orders in 1635 and further fortified by Vauban in the following century. It was here that the famous Man in the Iron Mask was imprisoned for eleven years. His cell faced seawards on the north-eastern side. The fortress also catered for a large number of other famous prisoners like Jouffroy d'Abbans, and Maréchal Bazaine who escaped during the night of 9th August 1874. Adjacent to the cell occupied by the Man in the Iron Mask is the Maritime Museum which has extensive collections of wrecks and amphorae. It huddles beneath the vaulting of the ancient Roman water tanks.

A signposted botanical trail leads to the heart of the forest - an hour and a half's musing in the Allée des Eucalyptus or the Allée du Grand-Jardin. Information boards indicate the various species - sea pines or parasol pines, green oaks, Australian eucalyptus, cistus, mastic trees and myrtle, clematis, and sarsaparilla.

A footpath wends its way round the island past the Pointe du Batéguier in the west, the Pointe du Dragon to the south, the strange mediaeval tower in the Grand-Jardin in the midst of the orange grove, the Convention Tower to the east, and back along the battery path. The walk takes two-and-a-half hours.

A boat crosses the Frioul to Saint-Honorat. This is an island of prayer, or at least of meditation. On it is the famous monastery founded by Honorat in the fifth century. On the path along the shore, any noisy or rowdy behaviour is totally out of place. You have to prepare yourself for the silence and the ruins - St. Michael's Chapel, the Holy Saviour Shrine, and, on the westernmost headland a couple of yards from a kiln erected on Bonaparte's orders to cast bullets, the remains of a hermitage. All this conjures up memories of St. Caprais, one of Honorat's companions.

And here we are on the south coast. You'll see St. Peter's Chapel, which was restored in 1964, then the entrance to the Cistercian monastery. Tourists are permitted to visit the Museum housing some interesting Gallo-Roman exhibits, and the church built in 1875 by Dom Barnouin. The buildings on the north side are used by visitors who come for spiritual retreats. The cloisters and monks' cells are on the south side and are not, of course, open to the general public. Don't leave the monastery without going to the shop where the famous bottles of Lérina are sold. It's a green liqueur made from over fifty different plants.

The tower built between 1073 and 1190, which stands in the water, served for many years as a refuge for the monks in times of Saracen invasion. An underground passageway connected it to the monastery. On the ground floor were three vaulted rooms where food was stored. The first floor contained the refectory, cloisters and chapter house. Another cloister, another church, two private chapels, and the monks' cells were all on the second storey. Some of the vaulting has collapsed and some of the walls are missing but on the whole

The Chapel of the Trinité-sur-l'Ile on Saint-Honorat.

Biot, the Fernand Léger Museum and its 500 sq. meter mosaic.

the building is typical of feudal Provençal architecture. From the terrace, there is a view over Cannes and the Alps.

The footpath goes on to the easternmost headland. The Holy Trinity Chapel built in the 10th century on a "place of prayer" seems to have preserved the solitude of the hermit up to the present day. To get back to the harbour, continue along the northern shore, leaving on your left the convent of the Sisters of Bethlehem, a contemplative Order which settled here in 1973.

VALLAURIS AND BIOT

These two villages are potters' havens, and each was made famous by a genius. Clay has been worked in Vallauris on the outskirts of Cannes since the days of Antiquity. But the craft was on the decline when, in 1947, Pablo Picasso came to one of the town's

workshops. Today, the potters are the masters in Vallauris, and some of them are veritable artists. In the Romanesque chapel of the former priory, the National Museum of Modern Art has on show a vast

fresco called War and Peace, made by Picasso between 1952 and 1959.

Biot, pronounced "Biotte", was a centre of earthenware jar manufacturing in the days of the Phoe-

A potter's workshop in Vallauris.

nicians, in the 4th century B.C. It was here, a few miles from Vallauris and not far from Antibes, that Fernand Léger bought land shortly before he died (in 1955). Today, there is a museum on the site. Its front wall bears a ceramic mosaic consisting of fifty thousand pieces of enamel covering more than 500 sq. meters. Fernand Léger designed it for the stadium in Hanover. The museum, built to plans by the architect Svetchine, retraces Léger's development from the Portrait of the Uncle (1905) to The Great Parade on a Red Background (1954).

While in Biot, be sure to visit the glassworks founded in 1956 by Eloi Monod and the 15th-century church which has two fine reredos attributed to Louis Bréa and Canavesio. As evening falls, take a stroll on the Place des Arcades, with its beautiful 14th-16th century arches.

MOUGINS

Mougins huddles round its belltower and is worth a stop to pay homage to the Virgin Mary and Picasso.

Mougins, a close-up of the fountain.

In the Chapel of Our Lady of Life (Notre-Dame-de-Vie), the Virgin Mary brought stillborn children back to life for the duration of their christening, because the ceremony opens the door to heaven. Votive offerings bear witness to the miracles performed here. Once they had fallen asleep again, this time for eternity, the "little innocents" were all buried in the same grave beside the chapel. The church was completed in 1656 but the bell turret dates from the 11th century. Adjacent to the

The Chapel of Notre-Dame-de-Vie.

A narrow street in Antibes old town.

chapel is a hermitage which used to provide permanent shelter for one of the poor of the parish.

Mougins keeps alive the memory of Commandant Lamy, the explorer of the Sudan who was born here in 1858. But the town is even more proud of having been chosen by Picasso as the place to spend his last years, on an estate filled with trees and shrubs next to the hermitage. The artist lived and worked here from 1958 to 1973.

ANTIBES

The former Antipolis, the "town opposite" Nice, was founded by Greek traders in the 5th century B.C. For many years part of the Grimaldi's estate, it was sold to the French in 1608. Antibes was a fortress at the frontier with Savoy and it still has its fine ramparts that were reinforced by Vauban. The castle contains the works completed here by Picasso in 1946. The church that was once a cathedral (18th century), nestling in a tiny square, has a beautiful Romanesque chevet and a reredos by Louis Bréa (1515).

A few yards from the seafront, the picturesque, almost mediaeval narrow streets once walked by the musician Sydney Bechet lead to the Archaeological Museum in the Saint-André Bastion. Its most important exhibit is an Etruscan wreck dating from the 5th century B.C.

The summer resort of Juan-les-Pins, which is famous for its Jazz Festival, is part of Antibes. It was created in 1881 and developed in the 20's and 30's thanks to the American millionaire Frank-Jay Gould. Nearby, in Golfe-Juan, the Emperor Napoleon set foot again on the soil of France on 1st March 1815, after his escape from the Island of Elba. A column commemmorates this landing and marks the start of the Napoleon Road.

Cap Antibes at the tip of the peninsula has some luxurious villas. One of them stands in a 6-hectare park laid out in 1856 by the botanist Gustave Adolphe Thuret. Tropical plants, palm trees, mimosas, pines, cedars, and eucalyptus have all found a place much to their liking.

On the Plateau de la Garoupe, the highest point on the Cape (254 ft.), is a lighthouse with a range of 44 miles. It was built in 1837. The Chapel of Our Lady of the Safe Harbour (Notre-Dame

du Bon Port) a few yards away boasts an impressive collection of maritime votive offerings and two masterpieces brought back from the Crimea after the capture of Sevastopol - a 14th-century icone and a precious piece of silk, the Woronzoff Plachzanitza.

On the Nationale 7 road to Nice is Marineland, where visitors can watch the antics of dolphins, and see a grampus, and a number of marine mammals.

A mosaic commemmorating Napoleon's landing in Golfe-Juan on 1st March 1815.

The covered market in Antibes old town.

THE UPPER VAR VALLEY

You can follow the Var and, later, the Cians, from valley to gorge and from fortress to isolated village in a picturesque circular tour some 55 miles long.

Leave from Puget-Théniers, birthplace of Blanqui whose revolutionary commitment was symbolised by one of Maillol's bronze statues, Action in Chains.

Entrevaux, on the former frontier with Savoy, was fortified by Vauban between 1692 and 1706. Adjacent to the ramparts is the Church of Our Lady of the Assumption (Notre-Dame de l'Assomption) whose tall crenelated rectangular tower stands out above the rest (1655). The citadel on a rock 439 ft. above Entrevaux controls the entire Var Valley. An impressive fortified pathway zigzags its way up to the fortress.

Once past the Grotte du Chat (Cat's Cave) and the rugged Gorges de Daluis, take the D 28 to Valberg, an attractive winter sports resort at an altitude of 5,424 ft. The Cians Gorges gouged out of the red schist take you back to Puget-Théniers.

GOURDON

In the vicinity of Gourdon, the Paradise and Cipières roads (Cipières was once a brigand hideout) and the roads through the Gorges du Loup provide some staggering views of this eagle's nest clinging proudly to its spur of rock. Gourdon, which lies at an altitude of 2,470 ft. and stands 975 ft. above the Loup Valley, has always been a fortress - first a Roman encampment, a Saracen fortress in the 9th century, and later a mediaeval citadel keeping watch over the coastline from Cap Roux to Antibes.

Craftsmen, lavender-sellers and honey-vendors have now replaced the archers, and the tourists have taken the place of the infantry. The 12th-century castle restored in the 17th century has been turned into a museum housing an admirable painting of The Legend of St. Ursula and a large number of naive canvases. The lookout terraces were laid out as pleasure gardens by Le Nôtre.

SAINT-PAUL-DE-VENCE

With its town walls built in the reign of François I, its Rue Grande running from the Porte Royale (Royal Gate) to the Porte Sud (South Gate), its 16th- and 17th-century arcaded houses, and its Great Fountain, Saint-Paul-de-Vence is an artist's paradise. In 1920, the inn-dancehall known as the Colombe d'Or was the meeting-place for the painters Modigliani, Signac, Bonnard and

A narrow street in Saint-Paul-de-Vence.

Saint-Paul-de-Vence.

*A game of "boules"
in Saint-Paul-de-Vence.*▷

Soutine. More recently, it was popular with the actors Yves Montand or Lino Ventura.

The Fondation Maeght to the north-west, on the Gardettes Hill, is a meeting-place for creative artists. The buildings designed by the architect José Luis Sert house an impressive collection of modern paintings, sculptures and tapestries by Giacometti, Miro, Chagall, Calder etc.

VENCE

Vence is less "popular" than its neighbour, Saint-Paul. Yet the ancient Roman township is very attractive and was much loved of St. Eusèbe and St. Véran, and by Dufy, Matisse and Chagall. It was also much appreciated by the wri-

ter D.H. Lawrence, who died there in 1930.

The mediaeval ramparts run round houses dating from the 17th and 18th centuries. On the Place Peyra, a fountain flows with the diuretic waters of the Foux. The old cathedral, built on the site of a Temple of Mars, contains St. Lambert's tomb, a sarcophagus said to be that of St. Véran, and carved wooden choir stalls with motifs that are sometimes lacking in reverence. They were carved by Jacotin Bellot (15th century).

On the Saint-Jeannet road on the outskirts of the town, is the Rosary Chapel designed and built by Henri Matisse from 1947 to 1951. It is a major example of contemporary religious architecture.

SAINT-JEANNET and LE BAOU

Nestling beneath the proud spur of rock known as Le Baou, Saint-Jeannet was for many years a smugglers' village. In the Church of St. John the Baptist is the crucifix that belonged to the parish priest from Ars. Note, too, a number of fine chapels, a Saracen tower, and the "wash-house" made famous by the well-known Old Mother Denis.

Walkers wishing to admire the panoramic view over the entire Riviera from the Esterel to Italy can follow the quiet footpath that leads up to the top of the Baou. Climbers, though, will no doubt prefer one of the two hundred routes, many of them sheer drops, marked out on the Grande Face or on the ledges to the south-east.

The Renaissance patio in the Château des Hauts-de-Cagnes.

TOURRETTE-SUR-LOUP

Tourrette, the capital of violets, has scarcely changed at all since the 15th century - a circle of houses forming the town walls above the cliff, fortified postern gates at the entrance to the town, and narrow streets lined with small shops. The church, which dates from the 14th and 15th centuries, contains a triptych by the Bréa School, and a small Gallo-Roman altar originally dedicated to Mercury.

CAGNES

The cradle of the present-day community, Haut-de-Cagnes, is dominated by the castle commissioned in 1309 by the Prince of Monaco, Rainer I de Grimaldi, Admiral of the Fleet under Philip the Fair. The ramparts still have their old gateways and machicolations. The inner courtyard, flanked by arcades,

dates from the Renaissance. On the ground floor is an Olive Museum. The first floor houses forty portraits of the singer Suzy Solidor painted by Dufy, Foujita, and several great names in

contemporary art.

The Chapel of Our Lady of Protection (Notre-Dame de Protection) not far from the castle delighted Renoir. The artist spent the last twelve years of his life in

Below and opposite : *The picturesque village of Hauts-de-Cagnes.*

On previous page : *The Espace Masséna in Nice.*

Above : *A panoramic view of Nice.*
Opposite, top : *The old town in Nice.*
Opposite, bottom : *The Promenade des Anglais.*

Cagnes, in Les Collettes, an estate with olive trees hundreds of years old. Today, the house is a Museum in memory of the painter, containing his wheelchair, brushes and a number of canvases.

The tiny fishing harbour of Cros-de-Cagnes is filled with lines of smacks known as "pointus". The hippodrome to the west, which lies almost on the beach, is the meeting-place of race-goers from all along the coast.

NICE

Nice, on the shores of the Baie des Anges, is the goddess "who gives victory" (from the Greek word Nikaia). It was a Greek tra-ding post as far back as the 6th century B.C., the Cimiez hill became a Roman colony, it was a truly Provençal town in the 13th and 14th centuries, and it remained the property of the House of Savoy until 1860. But Nice is a French town that was "launched" by the British. In 1824, Reverend Lewis Way marked out a footpath along the shore - it became the "Promenade des Anglais". Today, it is lined by luxury hotels like the Négresco designed by the architect Niermans, villas (the one built c. 1900 that once belonged to Masséna's grandson has now been turned into a museum), and the Palais de la Méditerranée, an Art-Deco casino designed by Charles Delmas.

Old Nice shelters beneath the rock topped by the castle. Once past the famous flower market and the opera designed by François Aune (1885), a labyrinth of narrow streets lined by tall houses runs between the tiny squares with their friendly cafés. You may come across the Lascaris Residence, built in the 17th century, adorned with statues and decorated by Carlone de Gênes. Or the former 16th-18th century town hall, now the Job Centre (Place Saint-François). Or St. Réparate's Cathedral (1650) dedicated to a martyred child who is now the town's patron saint. Or, finally, St. Rita's Chapel dedicated to the famous 15th-century Italian mystic.

The Place Masséna.

A flight of steps clings to the 300-foot wall of rock. The Allée Aragon runs alongside the cemetery where Gambetta is buried and along the foot of a manmade waterfall. At the top of the hill, archaeological digs uncovered the remains of the old St. Mary's Cathedral and of some ancient temples. On the eastern side of the hill, a flight of steps leads down to the harbour dug between 1750 and 1830 out of the former mouth of the R.Paillon.

To return to the town centre, cross the Place Garibaldi which has a decidedly Piedmont appearance, the Promenade du Paillon with its hanging gardens, the Place Masséna laid out in the 19th

century to plans drawn up by the architect Vernier, and finally the Albert I Gardens whose palm trees are planted in 28 inches of earth over a concrete slab.

Nice is the land of churches and Penitents, among them the Baroque Misericord Chapel built by Guarini in 1740 for the Black Penitents, Le Gesu Church with its amazing sacristy, the Church of St. Martin and St. Augustin where Luther is believed to have said Mass in 1510, or the Russian Orthodox Cathedral which houses the icone of Our Lady of Kazan.

*The market in
the old town in Nice.*

Nice is also the land of art. The Jules Chéret Museum, for example, has paintings by Vanloo, Boudin, Dufy, and Van Dongen and a fine collection of ceramics by Picasso. The Museum of Naive Art has six hundred works gifted by Anatole Jakovsky.

But Nice is above all the land of the "salade niçoise", fun and the Carnival.

CIMIEZ

Cimiez stands just over a mile from the harbour on a hilltop overlooking Nice. It is an aristocratic district where Queen Victoria liked to stay. It is also the ancient heart of the region, for the Romans made the hillfort their county town, a military encampment and a holiday resort.

Archaeological digs have uncovered numerous remains of the Cemenelum destroyed by the Lombards in 575 A.D. It is thought that the saints Pons, Nazaire and Celse were martyred

Cimiez : the Roman ruins.

in the arena here. The Roman baths form a remarkably well-preserved group of buildings that are unique in France. The baths on the northern side were reserved for dignitaries. The cold room is almost intact, as is the cold bath chamber which is so large that for many years it was believed to be a Temple of Apollo. The eastern baths were open to the general public. The western baths were reserved for women and were refurbished as a church and baptistery by the early Christians.

The Villa des Arènes, which was built in the 17th century, houses two museums. The Archaeology Museum contains some fine statuettes e.g. the Mont Bego warrior, models of graves, Roman jewellery and Greek vases. The Matisse Museum has 150 sketches and some thirty canvases including Still Life with Harmonium (1900), Odalisque with the Red Coffer (1926) and Blue Nude (1952).

As an episcopal see from the 3rd to the 5th centuries, and the

site chosen by Franciscans for a monastery from 1546 onwards, Cimiez has great religious importance. The south side of the white marble Cross on the Place de l'Eglise depicts a crucified seraphim which appeared to St. Francis when he received the stigmata. The steps of Notre-Dame Church are said to come from the ruins of the Temple of Diana built on this spot. The entrance and West Front, both built in 1845, are in the "Troubadour Gothic" style. The interior is unusual for the richness of the painting on its vaulted roof, for the ornateness of the reredos behind the High Altar, and especially for three masterpieces by the Nice School - the Pietà by Louis Bréa (1475) on the right as you enter, the Crucifixion also by Louis Bréa (1512) on the left of the chancel, and The Descent from the Cross in the third chapel at the end on the right attributed to Antoine Bréa, Louis' brother.

The sacristy, the chapel where St. Victoire's relics are displayed, and the walls of some of the cells

The village of Utelle.

are decorated with mysterious paintings that may have some connection with alchemy.

The small cloisters and huge gardens planted with orange trees are havens of peace above the hustle and bustle of Nice.

Halfway between the hill and "Babazouk" (the "old town" in the Nice dialect) is the Marc Chagall Museum which houses the finest collection of the artist's work to be seen anywhere. The tapestry, mosaic, and canvases are all concerned with the "Biblical Message".

LUCÉRAM

Perched high above a sheer wall of rock, Lucéram is still very much a mediaeval village with its alleyways crossed by small bridges, the remains of fortifications etc.

Sainte-Marguerite (St.Margaret's Church) is well worth a visit. Built in 1487 and restored in 1763, it contains five masterpieces by the Primitive School of Nice (reredos by Jean Canavesio, Louis Bréa etc.), and a quite exceptional treasure, the most outstanding

item being a chased silver reliquary dating from the 16th century representing Margaret "Issuant" from the dragon that had devoured her.

UTELLE

High above the village of Utelle on a bare outcrop of rock some 3,900 ft. above sea level stands the chapel of Notre-Dame-des-Miracles, which is one of the holy places in the Nice region. Pilgrims have been flocking to the chapel

The entrance to the Vésubie Gorge.

Peillon, a veritable eagle's nest. ▷

on the second Sunday after Easter, on Whitmonday, on 15th August and on 8th September, ever since, in 850 A.D., three Spanish seaman were guided to Utelle by a star after being miraculously saved from a storm.

On a 3 sq. meter patch of sandy ground some 100 yds. from the modest chapel containing the statue of the Virgin Mary, the faithful pick up small grey stones in the shape of stars which have been left there by the Virgin Mary during the nights preceding the pilgrimages. These tiny stars are, in fact, the remains of maritime fossils

called crinoids, and are reminders of the days when the ocean covered the entire area, some one hundred and fifty million years ago.

SAINT-MARTIN-DE-VESUBIE

Saint-Martin-de-Vésubie is in the heart of the Mercantour region, "Nice's Switzerland", where the mountains are almost 10,000 ft. high. Saint-Martin, where people come to take the waters or to enjoy mountain climbing, huddles on a rocky crest at

the confluence of the two torrents that form the R.Vésubie - the Boréon and the Madone de Fenestre. The Rue du Docteur-Cagnoli, which runs right through the village from north to south, is divided in two by a small canal called the "Gargouille".

The church built by the Knights Templar houses the Fenestra Madonna. On 2nd July, the wooden statue dating from the 8th or 12th century, is processed up to its sanctuary on the mountainside, 5,213 ft. up. It remains there until mid-September.

Saint-Martin-de-Vésubie is the

starting point of numerous walks. The Boréon Route, for example, snakes its way through the pine forest, following the torrent and its magnificent waterfalls. Those keen on regional food will also be sure to enjoy the trouts and fresh goats' cheeses, as well as the ewe's milk cheeses.

PEILLON

Peillon is one of the most spectacular villages in France. Perched on a spur of rock with an altitude of over 1,200 ft. it cannot be reached by car. Steep steps break up the narrow streets, and the houses clinging onto the rock look like cave dwellings. Everything leads up to the church at the top of the village where the castle and keep used to stand.

The White Penitents' Chapel (15th-16th century) boasts some fine frescoes by Jean Canavesio.

EZE

Eze is a fascinating hilltop village looking disdainfully down from its 1,388 ft. on the corniches, or scenic roads, of the French Riviera from Cap Ferrat to Monaco. Huddled on its outcrop of rock and protected by a double fortified gateway, the old town that was so beloved of George Sand adds all the charm of mediaeval houses to the luxury of high-class restoration. The Tropical Gardens will awaken many a fantasy. And the vaulted alleys, often broken up by flights of steps, have the labyrinthine layout of initiatory pathways.

Near Les Riquiers Castle, the White Penitents' Chapel has a wooden statue of Christ called "Christ of the Black Death" (1258). He is "crowned" with a skull and crossbones. An inscription reminds visitors that "As you

The village of Eze on its steep outcrop of rock.

are, so I was ; as I am, so you shall be." As you leave the village, you will see a picturesque path that leads down to the sea. In autumn 1883, Nietzsche could often be seen strolling along this path as he meditated on the eternal return and on the superman found in "Thus spake Zarathustra".

NOTRE-DAME-DE-LAGHET

In Italian, Laghet means "small lake". Legend has it that a statue of the Virgin Mary was seen floating on the lake one day. As soon as the statue had been brought ashore, the water receded and a chapel was built. A few centuries later, c. 1625, the abandoned chapel was little more than a ruin. On hearing somebody sobbing, a shepherd discovered the statue of the Virgin Mary among the ruins ; her eyes were full of tears.

The chapel was restored and

Notre-Dame-de-Laghet.

the Virgin Mary placed above the High Altar. Miracles were legion. In the 1660's, Duke Charles-Emmanuel II of Savoy came in person to give the chapel a solid gold statue of the Infant Jesus. The statue was the same size as the baby his wife had just borne him. The four annual pilgrimages, at Holy Trinity, St.Peter's Day (29th June), the Feast of Our Lady of Mount Carmel (16th July) and of course at Christmas, attracted crowds of people from Nice and Monaco. Disused crutches bear witness to the miracles performed here. There are so many votive offerings that some of them are even hung on the arches of the bridges.

LA TURBIE

The Trophée des Alpes, which dominates the partly mediaeval village of La Turbie, was erected in 6 B.C. to commemmorate Caesar Augustus' victories over the local tribes. The colossal statue of the emperor that once stood at the top culminated at more than 160

Villefranche.

On previous page : *The Villa Ile-de-France, now the Ephrussi de Rothschild Foundation.*

ft. It has now disappeared and all that remains of the monument are some impressive ruins that have been skilfully restored. It was here in the days of Antiquity that Apollo revealed to husbands and wives alike the unfaithfulness of their partners.

The Rue du Comte de Cessole, which leads up to the Trophée, is an evocative reminder of the ancient Roman road known as Julia Augusta which ran from Italy to Gaul. It passes close to the square in front of St.Michael the Archangel, a Baroque church built in the second half of the 18th century. It boasts two paintings by Vanloo and a communion table made of onyx and agate.

SAINT-JEAN-CAP-FERRAT VILLEFRANCHE BEAULIEU

King Leopold II of Belgium used to stay at the Villa des Cèdres, Somerset Maugham favoured the Villa Mauresque, Isadora Duncan the Château des Rochers, and Jean Cocteau the Villa Santo Sospir. Béatrice de Rothschild-Ephrussi's imagination produced the Villa Ile-de-France, which resembles an Italian palace in a garden paradise. It houses an outstanding collection of Sèvres and Meissen porcelain.

In stark contrast, at the Pointe Saint-Hospice, a small chapel ser-

ves as a swift reminder that, in the 6th century, the hermit Hospice lived here in solitude and absolute poverty. To the right of the chapel is a huge bronze statue of the Virgin Mary 37 ft. high, which keeps watch over the sea and protects seamen. At the very tip of the headland is a lighthouse. From the top of its 165 steps, there is an unforgettable panoramic view.

The guardians of the Saint-Jean-Cap-Ferrat peninsula, Villefranche and Beaulieu, are two pleasant seaside resorts lying languidly against a semicircular backdrop of hills. Villefranche is just the place for a gentle stroll, with its labyrinth of narrow streets like the roofed Rue Obscure. St. Peter's Chapel, which was for many years used by fishermen to hang up their nets, was decorated in 1957 by Jean Cocteau. Beaulieu is famous for its Black Madonna and for the Villa Kerylos, a copy by the architect Pontremoli of a sumptuous residence from the days of Ancient Greece.

PRINCIPALITY OF MONACO

The Principality of Monaco belongs to the Grimaldi family and is a sovereign state that is only half the size of an arrondissement in Paris. It includes Monaco itself, standing on its rock, the industrial estate of Fontvieille to the west, the harbour at La Condamine, and the gamblers' haven, Monte-Carlo. People have been playing for high stakes here since Charles III first had the idea of creating a casino in

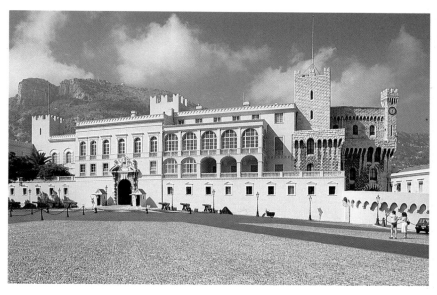

Monaco : the Princes' Palace.

1856. The Grimaldis were almost ruined at that time, but they soon became prosperous once more. Monaco's population pay no taxes and the fiscal advantages attract many foreign companies. The tiny territory bristles with

Overleaf : *A general view of Monaco harbour.*

A room in the Oceanographic Museum.

skyscrapers built one above the other up the hillside.

A visit to the Monaco Rock starts with the Oceanographic Museum built on a sheer wall of rock above the sea to designs by the architect Delafortrie and inaugurated in 1911 by Prince Albert I. This is the domain of the aquariums and underwater exploration made famous by Commandant Cousteau.

Two hundred yards from the Museum is the Neo-Romanesque cathedral built at the end of last century, the burial place of the royal family.

The palace is a little further on, on the site of the mediaeval castle of which all that remains is the Serravalle Tower to the west and the east curtain wall dating from the 13th century. The monumental gateway built in 1672 opens onto the main courtyard paved with pebbles. A white marble staircase leads up to the famous Hercules Gallery decorated by Ferrari (1552). The Throne Room and the main apartments provide a sumptuous setting for official receptions.

The Napoleon Museum in one wing of the palace houses a large collection of memorabilia relating to the Emperor, among them the Little Corporal's hat.

Above Fontvieille, clinging onto the cliff face, are the Tropical Gardens laid out by Louis Notari. It is a fascinating place for a stroll between semi-desert thorn bushes - cactus, euphorbia, and cereus. The surrounding rock is full of caves that were once inhabited. The Observatory Caves, in which limestone concretions provide a fantastic natural decor, open onto the Gardens. Finds made during archaeological digs can be seen in the Museum of Prehistoric Anthropology.

Monte-Carlo is the setting for the Société des Bains de Mer (Sea-bathing Company), gaming,

The casino in Monte-Carlo.

The tropical gardens.

luxury hotels, high-class shops, and leisure complexes built partially on reclaimed land. The west section of the casino, which is the oldest part (1878-79) was designed by Charles Garnier. In the Europe Salon, Americas Salon, Salon of the Graces, and the Touzet and François Médecin Rooms, everything is gold and stucco, a fitting background for roulette.

The wonderful theatre designed by Garnier has been graced by the greatest artists of all time - Sarah Bernhardt, Caruso, Lifar and Nijinski.

Charles Garnier was also the architect of the villa which today houses the collections of dolls and automatons belonging to the National Museum of Monaco.

ROQUEBRUNE
CAP-MARTIN

The 10th-century keep clinging onto its rock is the heart of the old town of Roquebrune. Commissioned by Conrad I, Count of Vintimille, it is the finest example in France of a Carolingian castle. Its last owner, Sir William Ingram, gave it to the town in 1921. A stone bridge, replacing the drawbridge, leads into the fortress. Despite major alterations, the Guardroom carved out of the rock, the State Room, the prison and the state apartments are still clearly visible. But the underground passages have been walled up. The terrace high up on the cliff overlooks the tangle of pink roofs in the village and the deep blue of the Mediterranean.

Originally, the keep and village both lay within the same outer wall. The mediaeval streets like the Rue Moncollet, some of them covered with vaulted passageways cut into the cliff, wind past patrician residences of days long gone. The square in front of the 12th-century St. Margaret's Church is

A narrow street in the old town of Roquebrune.

Cap Martin.

The picturesque town of Menton.

covered with a pebble mosaic made by the local people in 1776. It was from here that Bonaparte, then the young Commander-in-Chief of the Italian army, sent his first despatch in 1796.

A wonderful footpath known as the "Chemin de Menton" (Menton Path) leads to the "oldest" olive tree in the world.

The Cap Martin peninsula is the haunt of the international jet set. Empress Eugénie, Edward VII, Albert I of Belgium, Gustav V of Sweden, Winston Churchill etc. all spent winters here. The luxurious villas screened by pines and mimosa bear witness to this pomp. A path runs from Cap Martin to Monte-Carlo Beach. It is one of the most beautiful walks on the French Riviera, filled with scents and views of Monaco, Cap Ferrat, the sea and the mountains.

MENTON

Backing onto the mountain, Menton known in the days of Antiquity as Mont d'Othon (Oton's Mount) is a sun-drenched town that is never bothered by the mistral. In some ways, this is Cocteau's town. He decorated the Wedding Room in the Town Hall and there is a Cocteau Museum in a small fort on the edge of the sea. A town of the Arts much

beloved by the poet Valéry, by Liszt and by Katherine Mansfield, Menton is the headquarters of the International Biennial Art Festival and the Festival of Chamber Music.

Holidaymakers crowd along

At work in the fishing port.

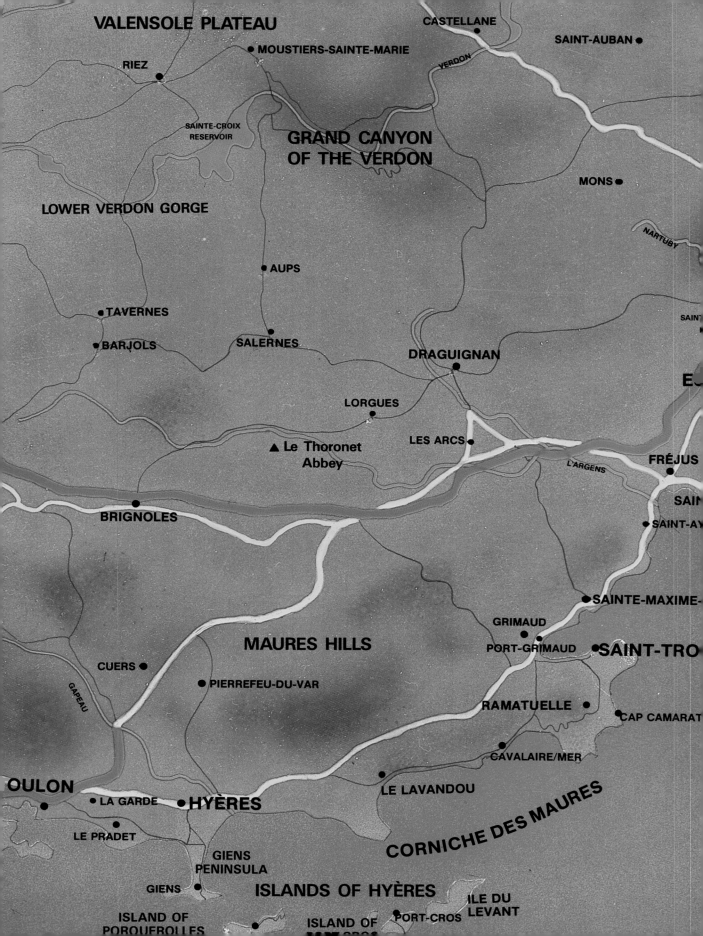

PUGET-THENIERS

MOUNT CHEIRON

MADONE D'UTELLE   UTELLE

SAINT-MARTIN DU VAR

SAINTE-AGNÈS

e la Vésubie

PEILLON

NOTRE-DAME DE-LAGHET

LA TURBIE

ROQUEBRUNE   VINTIMILLE

MENTON   BORDIGHERA

BEAUSOLEIL   CAP MARTIN

GOURDON

TOURETTE   SAINT-PAUL

CIMIEZ

EZE

MONTE-CARLO

MONACO

BEAULIEU

NICE

VILLEFRANCHE

CAGNES

St-JEAN-CAP-FERRAT

ASSE

CORNICHES DE LA RIVIERA

MOUGINS

VALLAURIS   ANTIBES

SIAGNE

JUAN-LES-PINS

CANNES

ISLAND OF SAINTE-MARGUERITE

EL

THEOULE/MER   ISLAND OF SAINT-HONORAT

ISLAND OF LÉRINS

HAEL

CORNICHE DE L'ESTEREL

ER

VAR

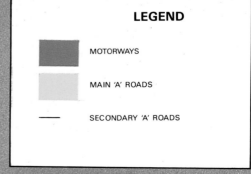

LEGEND

MOTORWAYS

MAIN 'A' ROADS

—————— SECONDARY 'A' ROADS

the Promenade du Soleil, on the fine sandy beaches and in the Biovès Gardens lined with lemon trees.

From the port to the castle, the narrow streets wear their past like a sash. The Rue Bréa provided accommodation for Pope Pius VII (at no.1) and Bonaparte (No.3). The Princes of Monaco once lived in the Rue Longue, the main street in the town. A monumental staircase leads to the square in front of St. Michael's Church, elegantly paved with black and white pebbles depicting the Grimaldi's coat-of-arms. The harmonious Classical facade (17th century) of St. Michael's Church looks like a theatrical backcloth completed by the Chapel of the Conception, also known as the White Pentitents' Chapel, which dates from 1762. In the summer, the square is the setting for some prestigious night-time concerts.

The fortress that once stood on the hilltop has given way to a nostalgic old cemetery built in terraces.

The Palais Carnolès to the west of the town was once the summer residence of the Princes of Monaco. It is now the Art Gallery.

NOTRE-DAME-DES-FONTAINES

Upstream on the R.Brigue, in a lonely valley, stands a plain 14th-century chapel that houses a real treasure. Its walls are covered with frescos painted in 1492 by Jean Canavesio and Jean Baleison. The murals, which are surprisingly realistic, show the Life and Passion of Christ. They have been compared to cartoons because of the wealth of detail, the vigorous composition, and the rhythm of the colours, all of which serve to emphasise the movement in each scene.

VALLÉE DES MERVEILLES

The tiny village of Saint-Dalmas-de-Tende leads into the small Minière Valley, which in its turn leads to the Vallée des Merveilles (Valley of Marvels), an impressive open-air prehistoric "museum". A whole Bronze Age community chiselled mysterious signs and animals into blocks of quartz. Tens of thousands of engravings exist at the foot of Mont Bego (9,334 ft.), the holy mountain of the bull god Bego, master of storms. This is the place for strange happenings - Val d'Enfer (Hell Valley), Cîme du Diable (Devil's Mountain, 8733 ft.), Lac Noir (Dark Lake), and Valmasque (Val des Masques de Sorciers, or Wizards' Mask Valley) to name but a few.

This is not a place to be taken lightly. You must be equipped with rainwear, hiking boots, food, and most important of all, maps.

Cet ouvrage a été imprimé par Aubin Imprimeur à Ligugé (86).
I.S.B.N. 2.7373.1153.5 - Dépôt légal : mars 1992
N° éditeur : 2482.01.03.03.92